A Chorus *of* Hope

CAROL ABNEY

DANCING CROWS
PRESS

Carrollton, Georgia

Cover artwork © 2024 Rook Feld

Library of Congress Control Number: 2024902867
  Abney, Carol
  A Chorus of Hope
  ISBN 13-digit: Paperback: 978-1-951543-25-9 Hard cover: 978-1-951543-26-6
                  Ebook: 978-1-951543-27-3
  1. poetry 2. hope 3. inspiration 4. grief 5. aging 6. learning 7. forgiveness 8. kindness 9. love
  10. perseverance

Printed in the United States of America.

DEDICATION

Dedicated to my precious son, Eric,
and to Steve, for your inspiration

This book was written in honor and
loving memory of Matt.

PREFACE

These poems are a "chorus of hope," written to give voice to the many different circumstances where one's voice might not easily be heard. The topics include growing older, learning to forgive, being a teenager, and dealing with grief or difficult family situations.

Tying all the poems together is the element of "hope." Even the poems about grief which speak of resounding loss have a small shimmer of light, that shifting of understanding at the end of the poem that leads to a new perspective and the ability to persevere.

As an educator for almost thirty years, I found that infusing the idea of hope as a thread through my English classes paid great dividends for us all, and that same thread of hope flows through my poems, as well.

In my classes, students learned to find those hopeful moments themselves. My goal is that readers of my poetry would also find hope in the poems.

Each poem is a combination poetry-story of someone's life experience. The poems share snapshots of life and tell each person's relatable—and hopeful—story.

Carol Abney
February 2024

TABLE OF CONTENTS

Part One:

Inspiration

Uncaged

Like the brilliant indigo bunting who,
uncaged, roams freely through the back yard,
finding a perfect limb to perch on and sing,
its image bursting through the kitchen window
in its infinite Kodachrome splendor—
a delightful, melodious surprise—
At times the words I long to write spring forth headlong
onto the stark, unadorned page,
and they feel perfect,
no rough draft required;
the words stream forth with a primal urgency,
and they are just the words that are needed
to heal my wounded soul—
I pour them onto pages
in hurried script
before I forget what I want to say
and how I want to say it.
Fly, words, fly, off the page to surround
other empty cages
with beauty and hope.
Take wing, though rough,
and smooth the jagged edges
of heavy burdens.

Part Two:

Each day, carry one another's burdens with love.

Brotherhood

We are brothers bearing battle scars on the inside.
We are brothers in a fight we cannot win.

"No excuses, no whining,
Chin up, don't cry, don't complain,"
The outsiders say.
But we, the brothers, know
How hard that is,
For we have had no one
To teach us how to be men.
Our fathers left us.
Our fathers abandoned us.
Our fathers decided
To seek "happiness"—however fleeting—
Somewhere else while large,
Innocent eyes shed tears
That could not be wiped away.

And the scars began to form,
And who would show us how,
We often wondered,
To navigate the awkward path of
Bullies at school, father-son days,
Making friends, learning sports,
Doing homework,
Deciding who we are?

While outsiders—always the outsiders—
Whisper condemning gossip,
Condescended to, scorned,
Never walked in our shoes, and
Laughed huge belly laughs at
Our mothers who fought for us
As viciously as soldiers must when duty calls

Trying to make sure we stayed
The good course,
And that the scars healed,
And that we became the men
That our fathers
Should have been.

Waffles

Two a.m.
Very early on a Saturday morning
at the waffle restaurant
with my teenage daughter,
all smiles because we just
left the big city lights behind
and are headed home from
an indescribable night of
watching her favorite band
in concert.

Could they possibly
know what seeing them
meant to her, how their
music brings her peacefulness
when the strange river filled
with too much homework,
uncaring teachers, gossipy girls,
body changes, relationship changes,
(really, the whole world changes)
overflows its banks and
spills out in tears on a bed
where she lies looking
at their poster on the wall?
Now life is okay.
She turns the music up loud.
She lets it take her someplace else, away
from the unkindnesses
and the difficulties
she faces each day.

But today
we are in the waffle restaurant
and the cook is talking about Power Rangers
and which one is his favorite
and how the green and white ones are the same
and at two a.m. the moon is lovely
and the clouds almost touch the ground
and the waffles really are quite delicious
and the hot chocolate warms her.

We laugh,
and nothing else matters,
except we have made it this far,
and we will make it tomorrow, too.

Mountains (a tribute to healing)
Inspired by Rook Feld's poem "I am a mountain; quiet as can be."

I am a Mountain;
Quiet exudes from every rock and tree
Along my well-worn paths
As sunlight filters from heaven
Through leaves and underbrush to
Warm my very soul.

I am a Mountain;
I am strong.
I could push through barricades
Of orange cones stacked three high
Surrounding me like an orange crush of emotional baggage,
And I would be unbroken.

I am a Mountain;
Climbers ascend to reach my peak as they hear their names
Whispered on the gentle winds,
And the whisper is of freedom from depression,
And the whisper is of resilience for eternity.

I am a Mountain;
Stronger than I know.
Many paths can be taken—
The Mountain knows.

Some are hidden.
Those are the best paths,
The most challenging,
The most rewarding.
I beckon wildly—take those paths.

Everyone is different;
Everyone belongs.
The Mountain knows.
The Mountain welcomes all.
I am a Mountain;
Quiet exudes from every rock and tree.

Why

Struggling to find comfort in the lumpy hospital recliner
sterile smells rigid pillows starchy sheets fluorescent lights
all stealing sleep which was but a dream anyway
on this terrible night of surreal scenes; my
eyelids are closed with their eloquent darkness
substituting for sorely needed rest
as next to me
IV fluids drip into a young, muscular, lithe body, now
lying still and quiet, occasionally waking
with garbled nonsensical words
nurses hushed and caring, trying to flush the toxins,
to rid the ruinous devourers of childhood.

I had come home late from work; another hard day on
the treadmill of existence, feet sore and mind weary,
saw my son sitting on the sofa; I thought something seemed wrong
but asked him if he'd like me to pick up his favorite meal for dinner
he smiled and said "Yes" so I thought all was okay
whisked myself back into the world,
returned to find his small room filled with people
busily checking his vital signs;
they held up a pill bottle: "He took this," they said
and my son's face held a look of remorse, sadness, confusion,
and pain
that cannot be erased from memory
and I scrambled for meaning and I screamed mental prayers
and I melted into a corner to let
the paramedics do their kind work
and the ambulance sirens wailed
please God, let him grasp life,
let him grasp beauty, let him grasp hope

And now we are here
these sickly pale green walls enclose us
I have to go to work tomorrow
I watch him from the recliner; I love him
I wish our lives had been easier
may our struggles be over
at least for a while.

I reach out to him
as I have so many times
angels hovering
so close I can
feel them
with us.

Random Words

My young daughter,
in her room decorated
with walrus wallpaper,
wears pink toe shoes
while lying on a green grass rug;
a luscious room.

She snuggles there with her books,
their worn covers comforting,
slowly turning pages,
reading random words
on those confusing days
when growing up

Seems more like a
glaring sun than
an addictive dream.

Sight

Dropped books scattered aimlessly;
Sightless people scurried past.
I stopped to pick them up for her,
Smiled gracefully, nodded, and walked on.
Today I loved.

Important places to be; important things to do.
Priorities, deadlines, ringing phone—
She needed to talk and the whirling business became
Nothing so that her voice could be heard.
Today I loved.

But soul on fire needing to be filled,
Burning and no quenching rain will come,
Seeking someone to fill the void—
Not realizing, not seeing the capacity was contained inside me.
It starts here.

Gentleness, kindness, goodness, and self-control;
Attributes of one in tune with the Maker.
Eyes closed, eyes open—blackness the vision,
But the soul sees light,
Only the soul.

Standing in the rain, staring up to Heaven,
Waterlogged shoes filled with mud.
Seeking solace, answers to questions.
Hands raised, arms open wide, palms turned up,
Feeling the touch, the embrace of the Eternal.

Today I am loved.

1 Peter 1:24–25 contains the phrase "the grass withers and the flowers fall."
This poem is inspired by those images and their meaning.

Forever

The grass withers and the flowers fall—
Torn stalks, wind-whipped,
Stark in their brokenness,
Bent, bruised petals
Once glorious in their splendor,
Now crushed under
Unthinking soles.

The grass withers and the flowers fall—
What remains?
Wise words discovered in
Ancient caves,
Carefully copied manuscripts
Inked with trembling,
Grateful hands—
Eyewitnesses to a
Change deep and
Monumental.

Though each day's turning
Brings decay to ripened fruit,
Though storms and tides
Wash landmarks into
Memories,
Though flowers fall
Like broken men
In faraway fields,
Though all men
Are like withered grass,

Yet this Word stands forever;
The Truth remains.

Sleep

Sleep is a distant radiant star
and I toss and turn
the covers twisted like a balloon animal
my mind tumbling thoughts over and over
like laundry warming in the dryer
and rest won't come because answers won't come.
The sleepless questions stack up one upon the other
throughout the night, a garish reminder
of the most intimate details of my fragmented life.
How did that novel I read in high school English end?
Am I now where I wish I would have been?
Did I remember to lock the back door?
Should I eat ice cream? It's a quarter 'til four.
Is my wandering son home yet?
What are some of my deepest regrets?
Throwing my legs over the side of the bed
I give up the fight, and pad
down the carpeted hallway
into the chilly silence of the night.
While outside stars quiver in eternal blackness,
I grab a warm quilt
and sink into a chair
to watch the romance channel
and forget why I am there.

Blue

"Like my best friend's shirt,"
I told everyone,
"That is how I am feeling today."
I could see their puzzled expressions as
they looked towards me quizzically,
then wondered aloud,
"How can you feel striped?"

Clarification was a necessity, though it
chagrined me to have to explain.
"The middle stripe—that's how I feel."
My voice was short and filled with woe.

"Aaaah—the *blue* one," they exclaimed,
their delighted faces aglow, having
solved the puzzle of my mood.
"But blue—why so blue?"
They clamored for an answer.

My inner voice said, "How can they not understand?"
Desire to end the conversation made me answer
with a terse, "Because my stuffed bear Scruffy fell into the mud."
Many little arms hugged me, and my best friend
Joe put his arm around my shoulder in kind solidarity.

Around the worn dining room table, my friends
(the ones that remain)
chortled at the retelling of our kindergarten tales,
as we all wore striped shirts
to commemorate the memories
of days gone by.

Part Three:

Each day,
grow older gracefully.

Winter

Palm trees sway gently
under low gray skies
as, strolling slowly,
with difficulty,
back bent and legs weary,
pondering
how the sea breeze eases pain,
how lapping waves bring
sweet memories of youth,
suddenly
a small smile creases
the lined face.

Walking on in windswept silence,
considering how many sunsets have vanished
into that far horizon—time does indeed march on.
Yet wind, waves, and memories remain,
sometimes roaring in like a torrential flood,
sometimes receding, gently whispering, dulcet,
like the foam that remains on the sand
as the water leaves the shore.
Flowing over aching, bone-tired lassitude
with mellifluous tentacles,
these memories, an aroma of times past;
are a sapphire resonance of bittersweet sound,
and a slow, wry smile
creases the lined face.

Up Stairs

Puffing a little from recent exertion,
I put down my grocery bag and ponder.
The stairs stand before me, insurmountable gray stone;
The groceries are a sack of bricks.
Once agile, I now imagine myself leaping, two stairs at a time,
up the long flight to the apartment I call home.
Reality takes much longer.

Now, if a fire happened to start
in this old building (I consider this as,
one slow step
at a time, I climb),
I suppose I would just burn
and call it a day, as these creaky
knees and worn joints won't bend, even
though my mind wills them to and the desire is there.

Young people rush past me, their voices ringing off the
concrete walls; voices filled with life, love, and tomorrow.
They don't really see me; I am the obstacle that gets in the way.

At the apartment, fumbling to find the keys to open the door,
I am greeted with walls of memories, pictures of loved ones
here and gone.

Exhausted by my two-story climb,
I collapse into a faded chair, pull the ancient blanket up,
its worn threads drafty, not soothing, then rise up,
summoning the strength to make a cup of hot tea.

As the kettle whistles and sings, I begin to remember
the cashier at the grocery who gave me the extra change I needed,
the man on the bus who gave me his seat,
the neighbor who waves good morning with a smile.

May tomorrow's climb be brighter.

My Painting at Eighty-Five

Like the characters in *War and Peace,*
we are not one-dimensional and easily digested.
Dynamic beings, we change and grow,
reaching out, trying to touch that bright star
within us. Just the grasping for it
brings strength and determination
and the wisdom contained therein.

Not twenty-one any longer,
As I celebrate turning eighty-five,
I am missing the former light spring of my step,
but grateful for the changes the years have wrought,
and wishing that those who see me as a picture glass window
whose view never changes would look closer
at the furrows and wrinkles and know

The frame around me contains not
an artistic still-life painting but a
flowing landscape—sometimes a dark Rembrandt
but usually a vibrant Van Gogh.

These furrows and wrinkles are the brush lines
that fill the window now with unexpected
pops of color; determination backlights the
painting, searing through the canvas,
bringing the new picture, the sensational,
uplifting, new me picture
into focus.

43

In her mind, that's her age still today—43;
That was a very fine year.
Moved to a new home, working at a job she remembers fondly,
Kids getting older, busy and involved.

But, really, 81 is the true number—
(don't tell anyone!), and
In that intervening "can it really be" almost 40 years,
Life's road has included stops for death,
Divorce, broken relationships among family, sickness,
Surgeries.

But there have also been peanut butter and jelly sandwiches,
Joyous family reunions, nights spent in deep conversation,
Game nights, potlucks, movies, vacations, and
Shared experiences of a kind that gold can't buy.

As she sits with family around the breakfast table, Madeline reaches for
Her favorite topic, the photo albums, and even though all of us
Tease her about it just a little bit, we enjoy looking back across that
"Really if you think about it" immense span of time—
81 years of life, love, overcoming, enjoying, deciding, choosing,
The beauty of an interconnected life
And a smile that still lights up the room
After eight decades.

And Madeline enjoys most of all the pictures of the little ones,
Newly born, who are just now starting this journey
As she is nearing its end.

Part Four:

Each day,
learn something new.

University Days

The gentle sun's first rays find my mind in mental knots,
concentrating in calculus class, listening intently to Dr. Levi
describe the beautiful complexities
of higher mathematics.

Menial work consumes the rest of my daylight hours,
a necessary evil to pay the bills,
while night brings yet another
excursion into the halls of learning.

Under the somber, deepening sky,
I dive headfirst into John Milton's world
of *Paradise Lost*.
Ah, the delight of the eager professor who,

Despite the late hour, longs for us to cherish
each turn of phrase and to write literary analysis papers
of such depth and perception that he can exhale and say,
"Yes, that's it!" and "Job well done!"

A great camaraderie grows among the devoted bookish owls
who have summoned the will to finish the entire masterpiece.
The work is rigorous, the hours taxing,
the goal sublime, life-changing—

To learn, to move ahead, to grow, to be better each day,
to walk across a stage with head held high,
to graduate to a new me with
incandescent eyes.

Royalty

Short dancing kings and queens,
deliriously happy,
eyes shining with love
of first grade and learning,
move in random rhythm,
their paper crowns askew
as they twirl and twirl
'til they all fall down
in a massive heap of giggles.

Watching from outside the circle,
wistful parents remember
the delight of spontaneous
laughter, the genesis
of glorious days, overtaken
now by serious introspection
and daily drama.

Breaking from these mundane certainties,
a silver-haired grandmother
begins to waltz.
A gentleman cracks a wide grin
and slowly, deliberately, two-steps.
"Look at me," he calls out
to the startled onlookers.
From the long school window,
streaks of golden sunlight
illuminate the scene,
and
an afternoon,
a day,
a life
changes.

Elementary

The teacher, though quite young,
had eyes lined with cynicism about tiny humanity.
"SIT!" she barked,
and the small, shy girl, tears streaming down her face,
arms clasped in front of her as a protective gesture,
slumped into a seat, pondering a world
where this person
(who she had so hoped would love her,
would show her the world in a different way,
would teach her to dream)
already disliked teaching kindergartners.

Perhaps the last night's revels were weighing heavily on her
and the intense headache left her unable to stand
the noise of children;
perhaps her husband was leaving the young marriage and so
any slight transgression from a child
scraped across the open wound of her heart,
or perhaps she had simply chosen a career
for which she was unprepared.

Whatever the case, with her face knotted into
a scowl, the teacher stormed away,
pulled the principal in for a conference,
etching memories for the tiny girl
that would survive,
a spurring impetus for her tumultuous future.
With her hateful stare the teacher returned, powerful, prideful,
a curt, "This way."

The little girl, now defiant, defense mechanisms in place,
stomped her tiny feet in her little girl shoes
loudly across the room
as she marched to meet her destiny.

Teaching Poetry to High School Students

"The next unit will be an introduction to poetry,"
the energetic teacher said, and the students' replies
ranged from *that sounds boring* and *poetry is hard* to
we don't like to write, and she smiled a knowing
smile of experience and said, "Trust me, you're
going to love poetry."

And she introduced them to *The Red Wheelbarrow*
and they were amazed at the meaning and craft
behind that small group of words; they
felt the majesty of Tennyson's soaring eagle and
Langston Hughes' exhortation to "hold fast to dreams,"
and by the time they had taken *The Road Less Traveled*,
they were ready to try this themselves.

And they started with the basics, counting syllables
to create snapshots of nature in haiku, then
they discovered that alliteration could create a
spooky sound in *The Raven* and they were sold on
this technique. When the teacher asked them to
say *Irish wrist watch* five times fast, sound became
something real and almost alive, and when Shakespeare
compared his true love to a summer's day, they were
ready to go to battle with their own metaphors,
and their eyes would light up and their minds were
on fire with poetic images and moments of great emotion
that now they could capture into words and call their own
and the only sound in the room was the scratching
of pencils across paper, and they would raise their hands and
call out softly, "Teacher, come read what I just wrote."

When poems form in our hearts and pour themselves out
through our souls, we know no class, no color, no boundaries,
no hate; we mold words into meaning and offer them up to the world
as a gift, our special gift, and the world heaves a grateful sigh.

Part Five:

Each day,
find a way to forgive.

Remembrance

Behind the kind, "How's your family?"
and the "I'll be praying for you"
lies
the secret email sent to the boss
intimating thin lines of wrong,
a stunning Brutus-level betrayal from a coworker,
a subterfuge worthy of Stalin
stabbing Hitler in the back over Poland.

You feel the icy blade against your skin,
but you need a roof over your head;
you need this paycheck.
You need this job.

They need the game.

You are a pawn.
Your move.

Return to Sender

The theft of my character
occurred at lunch.
This should be the hour
of friendship, reminiscing,
of happy memories as
we eat, drink, and conspire,
with laughter filling
the light air.

Yet a witness came
forward to describe
how a polluted soul
had cursed my name
in whispered furtive conversations
with those I considered friends.

Everyone gawked at the
roadside rubble
of my soul cut open
by the scathing words
of a young dilettante
scouting her way to her future
by stepping on my weary back.

Before There Were All-Night Pharmacies

The young pharmacist,
handsome, ready for a night on the town,
looked at the clock anxiously
as he counted out pills—
it was cold and flu season—
the pharmacy closed at nine p.m.

Soon he would lock the big metal gate
that barred him from customers.
He would hurry to meet his friends;
he had been thinking about it all day.

At 8:55, a woman walked in quickly,
having just left the after-hours
pediatrician's office
with her two small children,
one in her arms while she tightly
held the other's hand.

She rushed to the pharmacy window;
the night had been long
after a hard day of work.
She handed the pharmacy tech
the prescription for antibiotics—
"My little girl's ears are hurting so bad,"
she explained.

The young girl's dark eyes were
filled with pain.
Her tiny arms clung to
her mother; her weary head rested against
her mother's strong shoulder.
The woman's son, a little man already, stood
stoically looking on as the tech
hurried the prescription to the pharmacist;

she knew it could be filled in the precious minutes
that remained before closing time.

The tech returned quickly,
her cheerful face now frowning;
she could not look the mother in the eye.
"The pharmacist will not fill any more
prescriptions," she said softly.

"But it's not nine o'clock yet," the woman begged.
"Nothing is open in this town after nine;
I have to work tomorrow;
my daughter is sick.
Please."

The tech wanted to answer, "Yes, we will
help you;" instead, she had to say as she
had been told (he was the boss, after all),
"The pharmacist is not filling any more prescriptions
tonight."

The tech's eyes once more questioned the handsome young man,
who glanced quickly from behind the pharmacy glass
toward the pleading mother, then looked
away, firmly shaking his head—*no*—
his friends were waiting, after all.

He felt a small, short twinge of guilt—
a fleeting, unaccustomed circumstance.
"So what? I have things to do,"
he said to himself as he turned his back,

And the tired woman, head bowed,
and the young boy, having to be strong
for mom again,

and the sick little girl
walked slowly, sadly
through the automatic
doors,
into the parking lot,
into the formidable night,
while the insouciant pharmacist
barred the metal gate,
raced headlong and carefree,
celebrated
and drank toasts to happy times,
as the children cried,
and the mother did her best
to comfort them.

Silver

Thinking back
To the spoon of my life
Ordinary moments
Become dull silver
And slip off like drops
Of water
Refrigerator pictures of smiles
Now stare back at me while
My guilt causes
My hands to run down
My apron over and over
Until my skin is raw
With wishing that
Do-overs were a part of
Life
My vain selfish desires
Overwhelmed any common sense
And now
Pouring again from my coffee pot,
I sit, elbows on the mahogany table,
Listening to the difficult silence
Of aloneness
And regret.

Girl

Do not be the
Girl that I was,
Shackled by insecurities,
Filled with desires
For that relationship,
That man, whose love
Would make me
Whole.

Girl
You can relate
To where I have been.
No father.
No one to hold my hand
Through the minefields
Of desperate wanting
Or to celebrate with me
On the clouds
Of jubilation
On those good days—
Because there were good days—
But always that insecurity
That comes from
Aloneness,
Abandonment.

Girl
Find out these truths.
Know that you are lovely
Inside and out.
Know that you are capable
Of more than you ever dreamed.
Know that just as you are kind to others

You deserve respect, too,
And walk away—
Or run away if you need to—
When disrespect comes your way.

Dear friend,
This road I have journeyed
Has been filled with
Words that tear the soul,
Jagged unkindnesses that
Find their way into hidden crevices
And stay there
And come out at night.

But girl,
You can put that right,
And I can put that right.

Erase those old memories—
Start new today.

Part Six:

Each day,
really see people.
Seek to understand.

Spring Tide

At the lowest ebb of the water's edge,
Dark blue, the water was, and cold;
I walked, and I looked to the horizon.

I'd had your picture for a while,
A memory from long ago, but I found it again
At the lowest ebb of the water's edge.

A reminder of laughter and love and youth
Of dreams and the future and discussions and books;
I walked, and I looked to the horizon.

The vision there was peaceful;
A full moon burning to light the way.
A new beginning was before us.

You forgave me, and your encouragement
Provided strength for every day
As I worked to reach the horizon.

Hold me, love me again like you do in my dreams
As I finally learn to love who I am,
As I work to reach the horizon,

At the lowest ebb of the water's edge.

Someone We All Know

While others walk on
Gleaming hardwood floors,
Inlaid marble, or exquisite porcelain tile,
Her floor is less sturdy—
A composite of discarded lottery tickets
Whose numbers did not win
And tear-stained pages that list
Her dreams.
She holds her head up high and
Walks with dignity
Yet
When everyone else is chipping in
For birthday, wedding, retirement, thank you
Gifts
She wonders how she will buy groceries if
She gives,
And how it will look if she doesn't.
She owns
One pair of dress pants for work, two pairs of shoes.
She rewashes those pants each night so
They are clean.
Yes, Goodwill clothing is cheap,
But there is not even enough money for those
Right now; maybe someday.
And maybe if she had a husband
He would somehow buy Bill Clinton's
Donated Goodwill underwear,
And they would laugh.
That is one of her dream pages.

The Goalie

Silvery and sudden the rain began,
But the goalie stood ready,
Game face on,
Small in stature but certain,
Knowing all he had faced
In life
Gave solid confidence
(Like David of ancient times)
That he could face
The opponent
And not be shattered.

When the opposing coach
Sent in Goliath
To score on him,
He would stand steady.
The rain could fall
(And the rain did)
But, hands ready,
He would stop the ball
Before it reached the goal.

Goliath could not,
Would not,
Win.

Wisdom

Wise beyond her years
Wild flowing hair
And ruby lips
Seeing truths of life
That others missed

Difficult to curb
Her disappointment
Her derision

When others not so endowed
With insight
Missed the mark

They should have listened to her

Yet when she needed direction
She walled them off

She floundered in a self-created
Box
That held a wise, world-weary woman
Who should have heeded
Her own advice.

Wish

She's standing nearby and lingering there,
Cheerful expression, tousled brown hair,
Looking inviting, looking at me,
But my fear holds me back,
Holds me back.

Conversations, laughter, questions, and books,
Respect, faith, memories, the courses we took,
Our time together includes these and more,
But my fear holds me back,
Holds me back.

Fear of rejection,
Fear of unknown,
Can't make myself pick up the phone.
Fear—will I change that sweet smile?
Fear—stops my life for a while.

Decision's been made—
Can't do it, I say.
Status quo's good enough for today.
Talk is stilted, tension thick in the air;
Can't look at her, can't touch her hair.

Brilliant the dawn of the day, sky is blue.
But there is no you, there's no you.

Ernest

Aware that night is falling,
And I am out at sea,
My wife, I'm sure she's calling,
And worried about me.

Things did not go as planned today;
The sea grows dark and cold.
Thought I could haul in a big catch;
I guess I'm getting old.

My eye is drawn to the glowing sky—
The sunset rings the earth.
Will I see my wife and child tonight?
I row with all my worth.

The waters deep surround me.
Dark now the desolate sky.
My passing hope, my fleeting dream;
I kiss my love goodbye.

Eric

To have a voice
that speaks laughter
with every syllable,
to have eyes
that light up with interest
when others speak
about their hopes and dreams,
to dance and not care
what others think,
and to find a way
to make it all work
to the applause
of the world as
quiet kindness and
humility emanate
from your demeanor;
that is your gift, and
all serious and sincere
people watch in wonder,
standing in
thankfulness
of you.

Birthday

Precious child
There is no father here to welcome you,
But the room is not cold and sterile.
It is filled with the sunshine of your presence
On this icy snowbound afternoon.

Your cry of welcome to this world
Brings warmth and life as nurses
Bustle 'round, thrilled with your beauty,
Amazed at your smile.

You are not alone,
You are never alone,
You are a singularity of purpose and light.

A Soldier's Dreams of Peace and War

My son's first memory,
he tells me, is of an
airport where I, his Daddy,
get on board a big plane to the
place with a different name:
Vietnam.

And my wife, far away
from her native land
where we first met, her
family still overseas, raises
our son mostly alone.

And in the sweltering tank
filled with fear and friends,
I pray for each day of my tour
to pass quickly,
but the tall, aching sun
seems to stay noon high
as I dream of her arms.

Surprise is the best friend
of our elusive enemy, and
in an unsuspected attack
we take fire.
Training takes hold and
the battle is soon over;
a Purple Heart will be
my reward.

Returning home to derisive
insults and marches,
still a very young man who
has already seen the

scarring reality of the best and
worst humanity has to offer,

I cradle my son tightly
and dream nightly of
running through a field
waving banners that
say *peace* and *love*, and
wake in a drenching sweat,
rising to do a job that
has to be done.

Me

Wavy hair
Worried frown
Dark eyes
Dark as night's next storm

Seeking
          stability
Two parents
One house
Enough money
No bill collectors
New shoes
Doctor visits
          if needed
Mama smiling

Deep in the cave of my soul
Dwells bright longing

Deep in the ocean of my need
Dwells desire

Cannot do this
Cannot take this
Need two parents now.

Words

In a belching stream of ugliness
volcanic words flowed over me
with razor sharpness, forming furrows
and rivets that calcified into stone.

You are nothing
You have no talent
You are a waste of time
You are worthless

Searing lava of deleterious diction
mountainous monument of unending misery
my small frame wilting
under the continuous stream

of *words words words*

sounding not the lyrical wash of water over stone
sounding the beating rhythm of manic drumming

run run run
nowhere to go

Now, still sapling young
yet ancient inside,
encompassed in a shell
of remembrance;
some have chipped the shell, and
some have smoothed the sharp edges.

Break through this rocky penitentiary.
Climb this tall orchard wall, and
like a modern-day Romeo,
renew me with your
words of love.

Kindness

I dream of horses running on the beach
Nostrils flaring, muscles straining,
Galloping straight ahead with purpose.
Behind are all my friends, riding
Guard—they have my back.
Landscapes pass by, people I know
Appear and try to speak to me,
But I gallop on, a singular need
On my mind, and in a sad, strange
Voice, I cry aloud for all villagers
To gather round and hear my decree:
"Kindness to all," I state loudly and with
Dignity. I am your king and I declare it.

Earlier that day as vulgar words rang
In my ears from the street corner and
The television, news experts talked
Over each other in heated rants
And the fashionistas railed against
How some poor soul could wear such
A terrible dress—*Oh, my, I had thought
the dress was pretty; what does that say
about me?*—and the right screamed at
The left and the left derided the right
And I could not ride fast enough to
Stop the tide of words, unkind words
That washed up on the beach of
Humanity like garbage and old syringes
And waste and strangled us like
Manatees gasping for air while plastic
Choked our very lives and—
Plastic—that is the very word I searched

For—plastic—that is what our lives are—
For without kindness,
We are fake, manufactured, unreal.
Plastic.

Janie's Road

She wove her way through the
fabric of life,
the contours of her days
like a long, abused
stretch of Georgia highway,
always hanging on
to her motto, "Whatever happens, happens."

When stepfather number three came into her
life, she took off running and didn't stop
'til she reached the county line where
she hung on to the stop sign like
a fly on bacon and watched the
afternoon thunder clouds gather,
large and gray, and felt the
first pelts of rain fall hard against
her skin.

Hours later, huddled there like a
wet cat, a fireman saw her and
said *ma'am let me help you,*
and those were the first kind words
she could remember in a long,
long time.

Because you gotta start somewhere,
and you gotta find a way.

Misunderstood

Misunderstood;
the one descriptive word I carry
on my back like a weight.

More caring and protective
than a mother wolf,
I am a prime example of
don't judge a book by its cover.

With more obstacles in my
life than the state driving test,
I try to remember that it takes courage
to make your own path, instead of
following everyone else's footsteps.

With food for those in need and a
couch ready for those who need rest,
I am a positive walking discount store
with a light blinking above me:

Roll back, roll back, protective
gentle giant, whose misconstrued
words fail and falter, but whose
heart is always in the right place.

Part Seven:

Each day,
be kind to one another,
especially to those with
grief or loss.

Missing Matt: The View from Here

I stand on a cloud,
The world insignificant,
marveling Heaven.

I leap into the arms of love,
no pain in sight.
Angels hand me celestial paintbrushes,
and I draw orange sunrises and sunsets
and novel cloud formations
and even gloomy gray skies
as they have never been seen before.
I am sunlight and rainbows and light,
and they flow through me, never ending
eternal beauty; my canvas stretches far and wide,
and I think, join me,
but not yet.

Below me tears well up and spring forth even as months go by
and rivers are made of the dark grief,
so I stretch the sun's rays from clouds to say
I am here, it is okay, touch my hand,
and below, arms are raised high
in anger and praise,
in frustration and loss
and hope.

The Coat of Mourning

The alarm buzzes insistently.
Groggy, stretching, my feet touch the carpet.
My morning routine, familiar, comforting,
timed to the minute:
breakfast, wash my face, fix my wild
hair that resists being tamed,
and put on lovely clothes, pressed,
colorful, comfortable.

But before I leave home,
the invisible coat that I wear each day,
that clings to me with no warmth at all,
that causes tears to well up at unexpected
moments, that weighs three times what
a normal, reasonable coat should weigh,
must be a part of my wardrobe, though
very few people know I wear it.

Sometimes—rarely—I tell others of the
coat, but it makes them uncomfortable
and so I try to live my life in a way that
honors what the coat represents.

The pain of suddenly losing someone so
dear in such a violent way—
I have no words;
I have the coat I wear;
it is sized to fit me.

Still Life

The gray coffin seemed small compared to his burly body.
The day was sunny, yet cold, and the
few people gathered laughed lightly
amid bright conversation.

A piercing wail broke from his sister,
now an only child, and it
filled the sky with pain.

The grave digger looked on in sorrow,
then down at the dirty shovel in his hands.

A stray dog galloped across the green field
and lay at her feet; her cries subsided slowly.
Carefully, the dog walked to the side of the grave and peered inside
as if paying his respects.

He stayed with her until she finally turned away.

Hearing Voices and Seeing Rainbows

Others debate theology,
communion, and speaking in tongues.
In his shining star life
faith meant being a loyal friend
and a loving son and not
letting the bullies and the haters
get to him.
His smile spelled love and his
gentle demeanor spoke forgiveness.
He kept a carved rock cross in his car
and an orange leather New Testament traveled
with him everywhere.
He prayed.
A lot.
When the torturous disease that
racked his brain funneled all his
strength into trying to defeat the pain,
the light that was Matt
still brightened a dark room with
muted streaks of gold
through the slats of window blinds
and you could touch it,
effervescent shimmering light
that traced its way across your heart.

Crystal River

Over the marsh, the mist,
a suspension of stillness,
has settled.
As the minutes wind forward,
the sun leisurely lends
its warming rays to the earth below.

Early risers are fishing
on the banks of the elegant estuary,
their poles dipping with hope.
Picnic baskets are open.
Children skip and run, catch sunbeams
with their hands, soaking in the warmth
of this spring day. The trill of colorful birds competes
with the chugging of boat motors coughing,
starting up a new season.

In the background, in somber formality,
stands the once hallowed ground of burial mounds
and ancient temples where mourning
voices still seem to fill the sky with sound
and jagged rocks like ancient tears lie
scattered,
and remembrance of the
dead is but a fleeting thought
for the living.

Part Eight:

Coda

Each day,
enjoy life with a beautiful
fierceness.

The Train Ride: Our Song

The metallic clank of wheels upon track
was like a whispering song, she thought
with sleepy, wistful longing.

Her peaceful seatmate slept, oblivious to the
passing green fields, opulent grain, overflowing silos
filling the small, square window panes with life.

The train car door slid open—
A young couple entered; their energy encompassed
the tiny room. The train sang its forward song:
clang, squeak, clicking on rails, bells, whistles,
a constant hiss, wind noise, the sound of brakes, all
the noises of train life, an electric hum.

They came together, two sets of strangers,
in the glow of the evening sun
and shared this glimpse of astonishing beauty,
surrounded by rhythmic mechanical sounds.

Couplers hold train cars together,
strong and flexible over rough tracks, hills, curves,
as the forward-moving moments increase,
and time moves people to new and distant places.

The moon is rising on the eastern half of the horizon,
waning evening light filters through
the reinforced annealed glass
placed in the metal outer carriage
designed to withstand pressure;
the moonlight encapsulates all.

Thich Nhat Hanh was a Buddhist monk. He is considered the "father of mindfulness." Thich Nhat Hanh explained the concept of finding our true home, that place inside each of us where we find connection and understanding, which allows us to be a home for those we love.

You Are My Home

You are made of ethereal stars,
Eternity is in your gaze, your smile.
The universe is inside you,
A glimmering star path
Of trust and respect
That shimmers like a silver staircase
　　　　Into my home, my soul.

Reverence is in your words,
Tears fill your voice
At any person's pain.
Smiles crescendo from your
Every syllable
When goodness like a growing garden is cultivated.
　　　　You teach wisdom, forgiveness, compassion.

How can I express
That you are my home,
That my longing for you
Transcends time, space, and all matter,
That you are stars,
You are sunlight,
You are shimmering in my thoughts
　　　　As my home
　　　　　　Becomes your home.

Life as it is today

Yes, Mr. Frost, I am
acquainted with the night,
yet I search within each day
for that thing with feathers
Ms. Dickinson so artfully described.

I watch as the sun stretches wearily across
just waking clouds in a pure blue morning sky.
Crisp air clads early risers with the strange
giddiness of being alone
as others still lie deep in sleep.
They of the morning watch the progression
of the day as it begins, comes to life,
unwritten yet—
no turmoil.

In distant mountains where
bubbling streams make mysterious paths
through underbrush, animals seek
nourishment and feed their young.

In empty offices, row after row of cubicles
fill large sterile buildings, lights still off,
copy machines humming, poised on the precipice of action;
outside, pavement lies still save for the occasional dull swoosh of
tires rolling towards destinations.

In a tiny home, on her knees, an ancient lady kneels
by a bright window,
her hands clasped in prayer;
she begins her day thinking of others, as
she always does.
It is painful now—
"These old knees," she thinks—

but the habit of eighty fruitful years cannot
be tossed away.

"Maybe to sit while I pray
would not be so bad," she considers, as she
rises with difficulty, moving slowly to get her
morning tea.

A few intrepid joggers have rolled out of bed
and into well-used sneakers,
healthy and hearty, they pound pavement, too,
seeking chiseled bodies, endorphins rushing, blissful.

The sun is a little higher now;
children stir, parents wake,
some giving hugs while others speak
with cacophonous, grating voices.
Not eager to embrace the day,
their brutal self-centeredness
pulls joy into a thresher and churns
it into a chaff of wishes that blows away in the
morning breeze.

Lucky the ones who, while choosing
morning clothes, exchange kisses
and greetings and
listen to the crackle of cereal
as milk laps the side of a worn bowl,
not wanting for
anything, content, pleased to see
the sun, waiting for its journey
of the day, eager to sit
at the end as it sinks,

The sky now indigo with flecks of
sultry pinks, yellows, purple and orange,
looking back with a "well done,"
going to sleep with a smile.

May that be life as it is today.

Monte Carlo

Dulcius ex Asperis: From Latin, meaning "sweeter after difficulties"

In the parking lot filled with people
We noticed nothing and no one
Except each other.
He lounged on the spacious hood
Of his Chevrolet Monte Carlo, and
His smile captivated me.
My laughter filled the air in response to his jokes.

How is love born?
What miraculous, magical moment creates
The bridge that brings one soul in line with another?

In the parking lot filled with people,
That love was born.
It crossed the ages, navigated difficult years,
Survived many rocky roads, bad choices, missteps,

And here it is today—still blossoming,
Our minds still searching for one another,
Our arms intertwined,
Our hearts walking together, still climbing.
The tangle of years, unknotted,
Now a golden string of guiding light,
Startling in its warmth and beauty.

How can it be that when love is born
It never dies?

We can try.
We can say it isn't love.
We can walk away and turn our backs,

But it lounges on the hood of our hearts
Spacious in its capacity to engulf us
In its immensity of longing.

Hope

As Aphrodite
breathed life into Pygmalion's
statue, so you breathed new life
into my broken spirit;
you gave me new hope.

ACKNOWLEDGEMENTS

A most heartfelt thank you to the following people, for without you, this book would not have happened.

You inspired, helped, encouraged, and guided me, and I am very thankful to each of you for making the dream of this poetry book come true.

Thank you to Dr. Eleanor Hoomes and Dr. Steve Feld for editing suggestions and corrections; to Kathy Abney for formatting, editing assistance, and help with finalizing the book; to the Carrollton Writers Guild and the "Just Poetry" group for encouragement, support, and feedback; to Rook Feld for the beautiful and inspired cover design; and to Dr. Elyse Wheeler and Dancing Crows Press for their patience and invaluable assistance in publishing this book of poetry.

A special thank you to all who seek to help those in need, who take the time to listen, to care, to be kind, and to help others find answers and hope even in the most difficult times. You are like angels on earth, and you are appreciated. You are "a chorus of hope."

Milton Keynes UK
Ingram Content Group UK Ltd.
UKHW041726010424
440420UK00001B/2